DRUGS AND DATE RAPE

Date rape happens more often than most people think.

DRUGS AND DATE RAPE

Maryann Miller

THE ROSEN PUBLISHING GROUP, INC.
NEW YORK

Published in 1995 by The Rosen Publishing Group, Inc.
29 East 21st Street, New York, NY 10010

Copyright 1995 by The Rosen Publishing Group, Inc.

First Edition

Library of Congress Cataloging-in-Publication Data
Miller, Maryann, 1943–
    Drugs and date rape / Maryann Miller.
        p.   cm. — (The drug abuse prevention library)
    Includes bibliographical references and index.
    ISBN 0-8239-2064-X
    1. Acquaintance rape—United States—Juvenile
literature.   2. Drug abuse—United States—Juvenile
literature.   3. Acquaintance rape—United States—
Prevention—Juvenile literature.   4. Drug abuse—
United States—Juvenile literature.   5. Drug abuse
and crime—United States—Juvenile literature.
[1. Drug abuse.   2. Acquaintance rape.   3. Rape.
4. Dating violence.]   I. Title.   II. Series.
HV6561.M55   1995
362.88'3—dc   94-37824
                                                                    CIP
                                                                    AC

Manufactured in the United States of America

Contents

Introduction

Mary knew about date rape, but she never thought it would happen to her. She didn't drink much and she was careful about the people she hung around with. So she didn't worry when her friend Jane told her John was harmless.

They had both been at Jane's wedding reception, and Mary drank a little bit more than usual. She couldn't tell how much John had been drinking. The whole atmosphere of fun and excitement seemed to excuse a little excess.

When John offered to drive Mary home as the reception was winding down, she agreed. It was even okay when he suggested they drive around the lake first. John didn't

You may think you are in control when you drink, but, by the nature of alcohol, you are not.

try to make a move on her, and it felt good to clear her head a little in the fresh air.

John was supposed to take Mary back to Jane's house. He said he knew where it was, but he asked if she would mind stopping at his house for a minute. He had to check with his brother to make sure it was okay to keep the car out longer.

That seemed a little odd to Mary. What difference would another half hour make at two in the morning? But if he thought it was important, why not?

When they pulled up in front of John's house, he asked Mary if she'd like to come in with him; he didn't want to leave her alone

7

8 | *in the car. Reassured by his consideration, Mary went in with John.*

No sooner was the door closed behind them than John made a move on Mary. He kissed her roughly and put his hands all over her. She tried to push him away, but he was too strong. She begged him to stop, but he pulled her to the couch and threw her down. Then he tore at her clothes.

Mary's mind and emotions were whirling. Why was John doing this? Why wasn't she strong enough to fight him off? Who was that screaming?

Just as John was about to pull her panties off, an overhead light flared and a voice called out, "What's going on here?"

The sudden interruption startled John, and he jumped up. Mary saw a man standing in the doorway of the living room. He must have been awakened by the sounds of the struggle.

Mary quickly grabbed her torn blouse, her purse, and her shoes and ran out the front door. She covered herself as best she could, holding the front of the blouse closed with one hand, and started running. She didn't care where. She just had to get away from there.

Eventually, Mary found her way back to Jane's house. She didn't dare risk a shower; it might wake the rest of the family. So she

Our instincts often tell us when we may be putting ourselves in danger.

settled for washing herself, scrubbing hard at all the places where he'd touched her. She felt dirty. She was scared and humiliated. She wondered if anyone would believe her. Would everyone think it was her fault?

She felt she couldn't tell anyone. She felt humiliated. She wondered if she was to blame.

But the sexual assault Mary experienced was not her fault. Sexual assault and rape are never the victim's fault.

For a long time afterward, Mary lay awake wondering why it had happened. She also wondered what, if anything, she could do about it. She was in a strange town among strange people.

Feelings of grief, shame, and fear often follow an incident
of date rape.

Even now, many years later, she can recall **11**
every vivid detail of that terrifying experi-
ence. Looking back, she can also clearly point
out the warning signs she wishes she had paid
attention to.

"I should never have gone with someone I
didn't know, especially at that hour," she says.
"And even at the time I thought it was strange
that he asked me to go to his house, but I let it
pass. If I hadn't been drinking, I think I
would've thought more about my own safety."

No one ever "deserves" to be raped, and
a rape victim is never to blame for a rape.
However, both men and women can help
prevent rape by understanding it better.

One important point is that there is
often a connection between drug use and
rape. As was true in Mary's case, in many
cases of date or acquaintance rape, drugs
are involved. The most common drug is
alcohol. The drug helps create the opportunity for rape. Often, the drug also makes
it harder for the woman to fight off her
attacker.

Until recently, most people thought rape was committed
only by strangers.

CHAPTER 1

Defining the Problem

*W*hen one person forces another to have sex, it is rape. But until recently most people thought of rape as an attack by a stranger lurking in the shadows. Actually, at least 80 percent of rapes are committed by someone known to the victim. Forced sex between people who already know each other, even casually, is known as **acquaintance rape**. When the attacker and the victim are in a dating situation, it's called **date rape**.

People used to think that whatever happened on a date couldn't possibly be rape. It was rarely prosecuted. When it was, the effort often failed.

In the early '80s things began to change. People started to acknowledge

14 | that yes, indeed, rape could occur on a date. Just because a woman agrees to go out with a man doesn't mean that she agrees to have sex.

Then, in 1992, we saw the trials of Mike Tyson and William Kennedy Smith. Suddenly, date rape became a household word, and it also became a highly debated issue.

When Is It Rape?

Rape is an act of violence, not an act of sex. It happens when one person forces another to have sex against his or her will. Usually, rapists are men and their victims are women. But sometimes women rape men, and sometimes men rape other men. This is addressed in Chapter 3. To be **felony rape**, the attack must include penetration of the woman's vagina, mouth or anus (sodomy) by the attacker's penis without her consent.

Sexual attacks without penetration are called **sexual assault**. What happened to Mary was a clear case of sexual assault.

Sexual harassment is defined as unwelcome sexual advances. Those include requests for sexual favors and other verbal or physical conduct of a sexual nature. Sexual harassment is most often

Sexual harassment can happen at work.

associated with work or school. Sometimes it is used as a condition for getting a job: "Sleep with me and I'll make sure you are hired." Other times it is used as a condition for helping a person get a raise or promotion: "I can do a favor for you, if you do one for me."

A person can be a victim of sexual harassment without being asked to have sex. One 17-year-old girl who was a waitress at a pizza parlor had problems with the guys in the kitchen. Every time she went back to give an order or pick one up they made suggestive remarks. Sometimes the remarks were really graphic, and she

16 | was embarrassed. Their behavior made her uncomfortable and a little afraid, but she had to do her job.

She tried to talk to the manager about it, but he was only a couple of years older than the rest of the staff. He thought the guys were harmless. She was just making a big deal over nothing.

She didn't know that it was sexual harassment, so she didn't try to do anything more about it. As soon as she could, she quit and got another job.

Sex with reluctant consent can also be rape. However, it's very hard to prosecute rape when it involves reluctant consent. Women who are pressured by vague threats or constant insistence often give in.

Perhaps you have been dating this guy for two months. He's handsome, fun to be with, and you don't want to lose him. He keeps pressuring you, "Don't you like me? What's your problem? Everybody does it."

Finally you give in, but it doesn't feel right. Part of you doesn't want to be doing this. You're thinking, "I don't want this."

Afterward, you feel ashamed and uneasy. There was no romance, no desire. It was just an act that wasn't nearly as nice as you'd imagined it would be.

Negative feelings about that act of sex

You do not have to sleep with someone just because you are dating.

arise because it is a form of violation. A woman agrees to something she does not really want.

If someone is pressuring you to have sex and you don't feel comfortable about it, you have a right to express yourself. If someone else does not respect your feelings, it may be a sign of deeper differences in the relationship. It is important for you to respect your *own* feelings and decide what *you* want.

Rape Is an Act of Violence

The statement that rape is an act of violence is repeated often in this book. We

If someone touches you in a way that makes you feel uncomfortable, it is considered sexual harassment.

have to keep a clear focus on the violence. Too many people think of rape as a sexual act. This has helped create some common myths:

Myth: A woman's greatest sexual fantasy is to be raped.

Fact: Rape is terrifying. No one wants to be raped.

Myth: Sometimes women are "asking" for rape by the way they dress or act.

Fact: No matter how someone dresses or acts, she never "deserves" to be raped.

Myth: Women who don't fight back have not been raped.

Fact: This is as ridiculous as saying that someone who doesn't fight back hasn't been mugged. Any time one person forces another to have sex, it is rape.

Myth: It can't be rape if the woman had had sex with the man before.

Fact: Saying yes once doesn't mean yes forever. *Any time* a woman says no and the man persists, it is rape.

Despite the fact that rape involves the sex organs, it is not sex. It is one person violently taking advantage of another.

CHAPTER 2

The Reality of Drugs

*D*rugs do strange things to your mind and to your body. Many people develop a chemical addiction the first time they try drugs or take a drink. You can also develop a psychological dependence. That happens when people do drugs to escape some terrible reality. The problem is that they forget for only a little while. Then they take more drugs.

Long-range drug use can cause a number of mental health problems. Some of these problems are distortion of perception/reality, mental confusion, irritability, outbursts of aggression, and paranoid thinking. Many people also suffer from bouts of depression that can lead to suicide or attempted suicide.

It is easier for someone to take control of you when you are drunk or high.

All of these reactions can increase your vulnerability while using drugs. It is easier for someone to take advantage of you when you are not in control.

The Most Common Drugs

Stimulants—commonly called "uppers." They include marijuana, amphetamines, cocaine, and crack cocaine. These drugs act on the central nervous system, creating the "high" associated with them. They increase the heart rate, blood pressure, and body temperature. Frequent use can cause heart attack and stroke.

Drug use can result in psychological and physical dependence.

Marijuana is sometimes listed as both a stimulant and a hallucinogen. Its physical effects are like those of a stimulant, but it has been known to cause hallucinations. This is especially true when it is used with another drug.

Cocaine and **crack,** stimulants derived from the coca leaf, are highly addictive. In the United States in the past ten years, use of both drugs has risen dramatically.

Methamphetamine has effects similar to those of cocaine. On the street it is known as "speed," "crank," "crystal," or "crystal meth." People who use this drug often "binge" then experience a "crash."

During the crash they can suffer depression, irritability, anxiety, and insomnia. In extreme cases it can also cause a psychosis similar to paranoid schizophrenia.

Depressants

Barbiturates—commonly called "downers." These are usually used as sleeping pills and muscle relaxants.

Barbiturates are highly addictive, and tolerance levels build quickly. Addicts need more of the drug to achieve the same results. Barbiturates are also extremely dangerous when used with alcohol. Both substances reduce respiration and lower blood pressure, which can lead to coma and death.

Tranquilizers—drugs used to relieve anxiety and tension. **Valium** is one of the most common tranquilizers. It is legally sold by prescription, but it is also available on the streets illegally. These drugs slow your body's functions and make you feel mellow. If you get too mellow, your heart could stop.

Narcotics—used legally as painkillers.

Morphine is one of the strongest painkillers. It can be addictive, and doctors are very careful in prescribing it. Many people have become addicted to

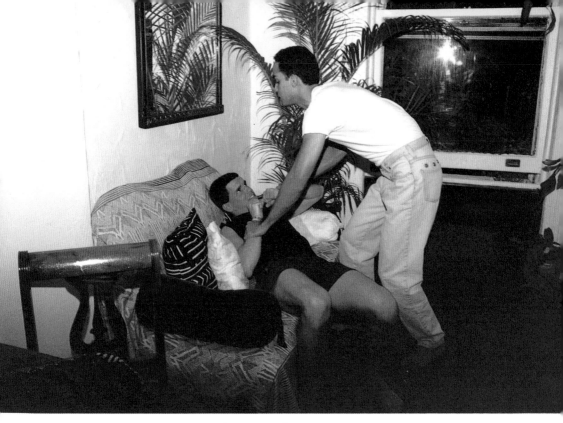

Drug use can make you violent.

morphine when using it to control pain after surgery or severe injury. Legal narcotics are often stolen from hospitals and sold on the streets illegally.

Heroin and **opium** are illegal narcotic drugs. People use them to get "high." The high can last up to six hours and is followed by a "downer" that can last for days. Heroin, like crack, can be immediately addictive. The longer the addiction, the more of the drug is needed to satisfy the craving.

Hallucinogens—include LSD and PCP. LSD is known as "acid" and has been used widely since the sixties. PCP, "angel dust,"

has been around just as long but became
more popular in the 1970s and '80s.
These drugs distort reality. They can
make you see and hear things that are not
there. They can also make you believe
you can do impossible things. On a "bad
trip" many young people die in accidents.
Marijuana cigarettes can be "laced" with
LSD or PCP without your knowing it.

PCP can also produce paranoia, intense
anger, and hostility. Some experts believe
it causes more violent behavior than any
other drug.

Alcohol—Some people don't consider
it to be one, in part because it is legal, but
it is. However, possession and use of
alcohol by minors (people under the age of
21) are illegal. So are public intoxication
and driving under the influence (DUI).

Alcohol is not immediately addictive,
but it does have immediate effects. It dis-
turbs the normal working of the central
nervous system. That's why people stumble
around and slur their speech when they
are drunk.

Alcohol is the most common drug
associated with date rape. In a 1985 *Ms.*
magazine survey of college women who
had been raped, 73 percent said their
attackers were under the influence of

One of the possible effects of drinking alcohol is passing out,
which leaves you vulnerable to any sort of sexual abuse.

drugs or alcohol. Fifty-five percent said they themselves were intoxicated.

A more recent study indicates that 90 percent of all reported campus rapes are associated with alcohol: Either the victim or the attacker is drunk. The same study reported that many students forget about safe sex practices when they are drunk. Of even more concern in this study was the rise in drinking at college.

Being drunk makes a woman more vulnerable to rape. Her responses are slower and less effective. Maybe her speech is so slurred that she can't even put her objections into words.

Drinking is sometimes used as an excuse for rape. Some men think "good" girls don't drink. So if a girl is drinking, she must be "bad." That means she's "easy" sexually, too. But there is never justification for rape.

Use of drugs or alcohol puts women at greater risk of sexual assault or rape. For that reason, it is important to be particularly aware of when you may be putting yourself in danger. It is best if you avoid use of drugs and alcohol altogether. But if you are not able to do so, pay attention to where you are and with whom.

If you drink, pay attention to how much you're drinking. You may know how

Alcohol is present in many party situations.

one or two drinks affect you, and you can stop before you get drunk. Drugs are more difficult to use moderately. You never know the actual strength of the drug you are using; it can vary quite a bit. You may think you can smoke one joint without losing control, but what if that joint is laced with a stronger drug?

Drugs and alcohol affect the attacker as well as the victim. A man who is drunk or high may be more aggressive or violent than normal. His judgment is impaired, making him less responsive to a victim's protests. *That does not excuse his actions.* However, it is another aspect of the dangers of drugs.

CHAPTER 3

Drugs, Sex, and Rape

*I*n an article in *Harper's* magazine (March 1994), Mary Gaitskill wrote about her experience with date/acquaintance rape. When she was 16 she was with an older friend in an apartment. A man came over with some acid. They all got high. The friend left, but the man stayed. He started forcing himself on her. She was scared. "I let myself get drawn into sex because I couldn't face the fact that if I said no, things might get ugly."

Things were already ugly. She was raped. The man took advantage of the fact that she was high and that they were alone.

Urging someone to drink or use drugs has long been a method people have used

30 | to persuade others to do what they want. Alcohol and drug use alters our judgment and weakens the inhibitions that usually control our behavior. It also weakens our ability to protect ourselves in times of danger. It is important to protect yourself. Listen to your instincts. Avoid situations in which you may be vulnerable. Some parties turn into unwanted sexual encounters. These encounters often go unreported.

Who's Vulnerable?

Anybody can be a victim of rape. Date or acquaintance rape, however, is most common among women of 15 to 24. Acquaintance rape is most likely to take place in a victim's home. For this reason, think carefully about whom you invite to your home.

There are some specific actions that can make you more vulnerable to date or acquaintance rape:

- Going out alone with someone you don't know very well.
- Accepting a ride from someone you don't know very well.
- Going to a party when you don't know the person giving it.
- Letting someone into your home when you are alone.

Anyone, male or female, is vulnerable to rape.

- Accepting a dare to drink more than you are comfortable with.
- Giving in to the pressure to do drugs.

Drugs can lead you into other dangerous situations. Some young addicts are pressured into prostitution. The dealer may force them into it, or they may make the choice, thinking it is the only way to make money to buy drugs.

Sadly, such teens are controlled by their drug addiction. Without the craving for drugs, these young people would not be on street corners picking up customers.

32 | If their judgment were not clouded by drugs, they would probably realize the harm they were doing.

Men as Victims

Men can be victims of rape. They may be raped by a woman or by another man. Like any other rape, it is a terrifying, humiliating, and violent experience.

A man's erection is controlled by the male hormone testosterone. When sexually aroused, anxious, or afraid, his body releases the hormone, and he has an erection.

In most cases a woman can't overpower a man and force him to have sex. Usually, the man is stronger and can fight her off. But a woman can, and often does, use a weapon to force him.

Men can also be forced to have sex with other men. In this case, rape includes penetration of the anus (sodomy) or mouth of the victim by the attacker's penis without the victim's consent. This kind of rape happens routinely in prisons.

Occasions of reluctant consent also happen to young men.

Brad

Brad was a high school senior and secretly proud of the fact that he was still a virgin.

Men are also subjected to sexual harassment or abuse.

Like most of the other guys, Brad thought Sheila was terrific. She was popular and flirted with all the guys. Sometimes Brad pretended that she meant it when she flirted with him, but most of the time he was realistic—he didn't stand a chance.

One day Sheila asked him to tutor her in calculus. Brad was thrilled. If they studied together she would see what a great guy he was. Maybe she'd agree to go out with him.

After the first study session, Brad was disappointed. Sheila didn't want to concentrate on homework. She wanted to flirt. Brad wasn't sure how to react. In some ways it made him feel good, but he also felt

34 | *uncomfortable about it. When he tried to get her to be serious about studying, she laughed.*

The next session went just as badly.

On the third night, Brad was ready to tell Sheila that this just wasn't working. Then she came over and sat on his lap, letting her incredible blonde hair brush across his face.

His body immediately responded, but Brad didn't want to have sex. He tried to tell Sheila, but she laughed again. She came on to him strongly. Of course, he must want it— he was ready. So, reluctantly, Brad gave in.

Afterward, Brad felt guilty and ashamed. He didn't tell anyone about the incident. How could he? No one would believe him.

Male victims, too, do not like to talk about rape. It's even harder to talk about being the victim of a same-sex rape. Men who have been raped by other men may question their masculinity. Can they tell their friends? They might wrongly be labeled homosexual. Being raped does not make you homosexual. It means that you have been sexually violated.

Many rape crisis centers now have male and female counselors. Any man who has been raped can take advantage of the help offered by these centers.

CHAPTER 4

Rape on the Rise

*I*t is estimated that one in four girls nationwide will be raped in her lifetime.

Only about 5 percent of rape victims report it.

Most victims of date/acquaintance rape are between the ages of 15 and 24.

Stranger-rape accounts for only one out of five attacks.

Rates of rape in the United States are among the highest of any country.

Less than 5 percent of rapists go to jail.

Available statistics show that rape is on the rise in the United States. It is also interesting to note that the age of rapists

Most victims of date or acquaintance rape are between the ages of 15 and 24.

is declining. Boys younger than 13 are
being arrested for rape.

The overall increase in violence has con-
tributed to the increase in stranger rape.
People are more likely to act out their
frustrations in violent crime than in the
past. The message in music videos, ads,
and movies that it is acceptable to disres-
pect women is also a factor. An impres-
sionable teenager can believe rape is okay
when his favorite band tells him that.

A general acceptance of sexual activity
also adds to the problem of rape. Sex is
too often seen as a "game" that people
can play any time they like. It doesn't
matter what the other person wants.

The difficulty in prosecuting rape is
another reason for the increase. Some
rapists believe they can get away with it,
so they are less afraid to try it. This is
especially true of acquaintance rape and
date rape.

Among the reasons rape is hard to
prosecute are the following:

- Skeptical police. It's usually the
  woman's word against the man's. A
  lack of witnesses or bruising or other
  signs of force make it harder to
  prove.

38

- Hard-to-convince juries. This is especially true if the victim had willingly had sex with the attacker in the past. Rapists' defense attorneys use the information to try to make the victim look responsible for the attack.
- Reluctant prosecutors. Rape cases are especially hard to win. There is usually a lack of physical evidence to prove the crime. The defendant often accepts a lesser plea rather than go to court.

Rape in College

Date rape is a growing problem on college campuses. Co-ed dorms and an increase in drinking are only two factors. In an article in TIME (June 3, 1991), Nancy Gibbs wrote that rape is an easy crime at college. ". . . Doors are left unlocked, visitors come and go, and female students give classmates the benefit of the doubt."

Drinking, however, is still the primary factor. A report by higher education experts indicates that more college students are drinking now than in the past. Forty-two percent of the students surveyed said they regularly drink heavily. The number

Insecure dorms add to the danger of rape on college campuses.

who said they drink to get drunk has tripled over the last 15 years. Many students drink every day or three or four times a week.

College freshmen are particularly vulnerable to the dangers of drinking and rape. They are away from home for the first time; they no longer have their parents around telling them what to do. With all this freedom, they tend to act impulsively.

They are also more likely to give in to the social pressure to drink too much. Drinking parties and binges become like a rite of passage. Drugs are also easily

Peer pressure exists in all groups, especially among teens.

available on campus. Unwilling students are often pressured into using drugs to be accepted as part of the group.

"The pressure is always there," says one student. "If you don't have sex you're considered a weirdo. But if you don't even drink, well, that's even worse."

This young woman left a prestigious

private school on the East Coast because of the drinking and sex. "I really loved the school," she says. "But I couldn't stand all that other stuff. And having to deal with it made it so hard to concentrate on studying."

Awareness Programs

Many colleges are working to increase awareness of rape on campus. They are offering programs to show the risks, promote safety, and let potential victims know what to do during and after an attack.

Despite this awareness, reporting a rape on campus can be less than satisfactory. To avoid publicity, college officials want the report to be handled quietly. They steer the victim away from outside law enforcement, assuring her that the matter will be handled by campus police.

What usually happens is that the man receives a lesser charge and few consequences. A man who raped a student at The College of William and Mary was barred from any dorm or fraternity house other than his own for four years. He was, however, allowed to stay on campus.

A recent case in Minnesota shows how serious the problem can be. Four women

Most schools promote rape awareness and prevention. You could talk to someone involved with these programs to learn more about them.

are suing Carleton College for attacks they suffered as students there. The women were raped on separate occasions. When the first two women met each other, they discovered that they had been raped by the same man. The other two women also had a single attacker.

In each case the assault had been reported to school officials and campus police. The men were given mild reprimands and released. Then they raped again.

The women charge that the school put them in danger, knowing that the men had histories of sexual abuse and doing nothing.

To avoid this situation at any school, victims should make their reports to the local police department. In that way the rape won't be covered up, leaving the rapist free to attack again.

CHAPTER 5

After the Fact

*I*n most people's experience, nothing is worse than the trauma of being raped. It is a tragic physical violation that leaves long-lasting emotional scars.

Thirty out of every 100 victims think about suicide after a rape. Eighty-two out of 100 say they are changed forever by the rape.

Victims feel fear, shock, disbelief, and anger during the attack and immediately afterward. Soon they may start feeling embarrassment, guilt, and powerlessness. Dealing with these emotions is not easy. Most victims need professional help to sort through their reactions and get past the incident.

"The effects of acquaintance rape are as serious as those of stranger rape," says psychologist Peg Ziegler, director of the Grady Memorial Hospital Rape Crisis Center in Atlanta. In an article in *Glamour* magazine (June 1993), she told authors Cindi Levine and Sarah Glazer that the effects can include nightmares, depression, and suicidal impulses.

A typical victim reaction follows a series of steps:

Denial. This takes place during and after the attack: "This can't be happening. If I just talk to him he'll stop. It wasn't rape. It couldn't be. I agreed to go out with him."

Dissociation. During the rape there may be a time when the victim feels physically and mentally removed from what's happening. This protective reaction helps the person cope without having to face the awful reality.

Self-blame. This is especially strong in victims of acquaintance rape or date rape. They constantly question themselves, asking "What did I do to cause this?" They convince themselves that it was their own fault. That is one of the primary reasons many women don't report date rape.

If you have been raped is to go to the hospital to get checked for injury, STDs, or evidence (in case you decide to press charges).

A victim needs to work through the emotional trauma of rape. Gail Elizabeth Wyatt, a professor of medical psychology at UCLA, offers the following advice:

- Understand that you won't get over rape. You have to learn to cope with how you feel about having been victimized.
- Blaming yourself doesn't help the healing process. It increases feelings of low self-esteem and powerlessness.
- Talking about rape can be therapeutic. Sharing your experience in support groups or with trusted friends can help you cope.

What if It Happens to Me?

If you are ever attacked, look for a way to escape. Scream if you can. Some rapists are startled by that and run away. It can also help to use force against the attacker. Kicking or scratching could surprise him and give you a moment to get away. Then run as fast as you can.

If you can't get away, you can try talking to the man. Rapists usually think of their victims as objects. When the "object" has a voice, it could make them change their mind.

48   You might also consider taking a self-defense or a martial arts course.

If all your efforts fail, and you are raped, remember it is not your fault.

Rape crisis centers and other organizations offer good advice about what to do immediately afterward. Call the police. Go immediately to a hospital. Do not bathe, douche, change clothes, or apply medication.

The problem is that most victims want to run and hide. They are not thinking clearly enough to remember all the advice.

The best thing to do is to call a rape crisis center. A staff member there can help you sort through the things you could or should do. The person is just a voice on the phone; you won't have to deal with people asking questions you aren't ready to answer.

The biggest decision you have to make is whether or not to report the rape. Keep in mind that if you don't report it, the criminal is free to rape again. Many rapists are repeat offenders, and your courage could save someone else.

From a legal standpoint, it's easier to prosecute if the rape is reported immediately. Medical evidence can be obtained at a hospital, and any signs of force are usually still evident.

Going to court is never a pleasant experience for a rape victim, but it is getting easier. In 1991, the United States Supreme Court made an important ruling in rape cases: Victims can no longer be harassed on the stand with questions about past sexual experiences.

In 1993, Canada proposed a new law defining consent to sex. The law also limited what could be said in court about a victim's previous sexual history. Judy Rebick, President of the National Action Committee on the Status of Women, says, "Finally we have a bill that says 'no means no.'"

These changes are happening because more people are accepting the fact that **rape is an act of violence, not of sex**.

CHAPTER 6

Playing It Safe

*F*or a woman, the first date is an opportunity to have fun and get to know someone. Men often see the first date as an opportunity to advance sexually. Maybe they won't "score" that night, but it could lead to something.

That is a conclusion from a 1983 research project conducted by Charlene L. Muehlen. She believes that the difference in expectations is what leads to the miscommunication. The girl flirts with the boy, hoping he will ask her out. He may think she is sending signals that she wants to have sex.

This points up the importance of com-

municating our true intentions clearly and
honestly.

First, it is important to decide, *before* you go on your date, whether you would like to be physically intimate with your date or not. If so, decide how far you would be comfortable for it to go.

Next, be very clear in what and how you communicate with your words and body language. If something makes you uncomfortable, don't be afraid to say so.

At the first unwanted touch, be direct. Don't worry about not wanting to hurt his feelings. Tell him plainly, "I don't want you to do that."

If he continues, get up and leave. If you are in a car, get out. If you are sitting on a couch, get up. Look him in the eye and repeat, "I don't want you to do that."

If he is restraining you, you can choose to use physical force to get away. If you decide to use physical force, *don't be afraid to hurt him*. Use your voice. Shout "No!" as loud as you can. A cluster of fingers poked in the eye, an upward thrust under the chin with the heel of your palm, or a severe kick to the groin or shin are usually very effective.

Sometimes sound judgment can keep you out of a difficult situation. Say, for

Parents can make great listeners.

instance, you are on your third date, and he asks you to go to his place. If you have *any* doubts about your safety, suggest a more public place. Go to his apartment only if you feel comfortable. If you do go, be very clear about what you want. If you feel uncomfortable, don't be afraid to leave.

Most of us have a sense of when we are getting into a risky situation. Something tells us to stop and think about it. That voice is called an instinct. Listen to that little voice in your head that is warning you.

Other Safety Tips

- When you are on a date, make sure someone else knows where you are going.
- Don't go out alone with a guy you don't know.
- Don't go to a guy's house unless you know someone else will be there.
- Avoid parties where you know there will be drinking and/or drugs.
- Don't use drugs or alcohol.
- Avoid guys who use drugs or drink.
- Enroll in a self-defense class or a rape-prevention workshop.

Double-dating or going out in groups is a safety measure suggested by psychologist David Elkind. He also says, "Young men should be educated to the fact that not only is rape morally and ethically wrong, it's also a punishable crime."

The Project on the Status and Education of Women at the Association of American Colleges has been dealing with the problem of date rape. They came up with the following list of suggestions for parents to discuss with their teenagers.

54 | *What to Tell Your Daughter*

- Do not give mixed messages to your dates. Be clear about what you want and don't want. Say yes only when you mean yes and no when your date suggests something you don't like.
- Avoid falling for such lines as, "You would if you loved me." If he loves you, he will respect your feelings and wait until you're ready.
- Be aware that the use of alcohol and other drugs is often related to date rape. They weaken your ability (and that of your date) to make responsible decisions.
- Don't do anything you do not want to do just to be polite. If you are worried about hurting his feelings, remember that he is ignoring your feelings.
- Set sexual limits. If you don't want to go beyond kissing, tell him so. Stopping sexual activity doesn't mean anything is wrong with you or that you "led him on." The sooner you communicate your intentions firmly and clearly, the easier it will be for your partner to hear and accept them.

- Trust your feelings. If you feel you are being pressured, you probably are. If things start to get out of hand, be loud in protesting, leave, go for help. Don't wait for someone else to rescue you or for things to get better.

What to Tell Your Son

- When a girl says no, it means no. If you put pressure on her or try to persuade her to have sex, you may be forcing her, and that's rape.
- Be aware that the use of alcohol and other drugs is often related to date rape. It weakens everyone's ability to make responsible decisions.
- Your desires may be beyond your control, but your actions are not. You can control what you do. Sexual excitement doesn't justify forced sex.
- Do not assume that a date's desire for affection is a desire for sexual intercourse.
- It is never acceptable to force yourself on a girl even if she teases you, dresses provocatively, or appears to lead you on.
- Not having sex does not mean you are not a "real man." "Real men"

56 | don't force women to have sex with them.

Putting these suggestions into practice will help you keep yourself safe. By making good decisions and thinking ahead about what *you* want, you will be in a better position to enjoy your friendships and keep yourself safe.

Conclusion

*S*ex is a wonderful expression of love that two individuals can share with each other. When it is degraded by rape, the victim is hurt profoundly and the victim's sense of self is shattered. Date and acquaintance rape is frequently associated with the use of drugs and alcohol. As a result, it is important to take steps to do something about date and acquaintance rape.

- We can listen to our instincts and avoid dangerous situations.
- We can support drug- and alcohol-free parties and events.
- We can support the victims.
- We can stop thinking of sex as entertainment or a game.
- Above all, we can respect ourselves and each other.

Glossary
Explaining New Words

acquaintance rape Forced sexual intercourse between people who know each other.

addiction Constant need to use a drug.

amphetamines Drugs that speed up the central nervous system; called "uppers."

assault Violence against another.

barbiturates Drugs that slow down or depress the central nervous system; called "downers."

consent Willing agreement.

cocaine Powerful stimulant made from the leaves of coca plants.

crack Crystalline preparation of cocaine, usually smoked.

date rape Forced sexual intercourse between people who are dating.

dissociation Feeling not part of an action or situation.

hallucinogen Drug that makes you see and hear things that aren't there.

heroin An opiate produced by chemical modification of morphine.

LSD Drug that produces hallucinations.

methamphetamine Stimulant with effects similar to cocaine.

morphine Opiate used as a sedative and painkiller.

myth Belief not based on fact.

narcotic Painkiller such as opium, morphine, and heroin.

physical dependence Adaptation of the body to the presence of a drug.

psychological dependence Condition in which a drug user craves a drug to maintain a sense of well-being and feels discomfort without it.

reluctant consent Giving in to pressure to do something you'd rather not.

sexual assault Physical sexual advances against a person who does not consent, with or without intercourse.

sexual harassment Unwelcome verbal or physical sexual advances.

testosterone Male sex hormone produced in the testicles.

tolerance Decrease of physical reaction to the effects of a drug.

trauma Emotional shock that causes long-range emotional and psychological damage.

vulnerable Susceptible to injury or attack.

Help List

Rape Hotline or Rape Crisis Centers. Phone numbers are listed in local phone books.

National Rape Hotline—202-333-RAPE
Offers emergency counseling for rape victims; gives medical information and referrals to local treatment and support groups.

SOAR (Students Organized Against Rape) Started by students at Rice University and the Houston Area Women's Center, offers speakers to high schools on rape awareness and prevention. To start SOAR in your area have your guidance counselor write to

SOAR
Rice University
Health Education Office
P.O. Box 1892
Houston, TX 77251

YWCA **Women Against Violence**
24-hour crisis lines available in most cities.

Alternatives to Fear

Offers rape education and self-defense for adults and teens.
>   1605 17th Avenue
>   Seattle, WA 98122

Prepare Self-Defense
147 West 25th Street
New York, NY 10001
800-442-7273

Alcoholics Anonymous
800-662-HELP (4357)

Narcotics Anonymous
818-780-3851

National Council on Alcoholism and Drug Dependence (NCADD)
12 West 21st Street
New York, NY 10010
212-206-6770

American Council for Drug Education
204 Monroe Street
Rockville, MD 20850
301-294-0600

National Clearinghouse for Alcohol and Drug Information
P.O. Box 2345
Rockville, MD 20852

For Further Reading

Benedict, Helen. *Safe, Strong and Streetwise: The Teenager's Guide to Sexual Assault.* Boston: Joy Street Books, 1986.

Bohmer, Carol, and Parrot, Andrea. *Sexual Assault on Campus: The Problem and the Solution.* New York: Lexington Books, Macmillan, 1993.

Brownmiller, Susan. *Against Our Will: Men, Women and Rape.* New York: Simon and Schuster, 1975.

Estrich, Susan. *Real Rape.* Cambridge: Harvard University Press, 1987.

Fairstein, Linda A. *Sexual Violence: Our War Against Rape.* New York: William Morrow, 1993.

Guernsey, JoAnn Bren. *Rape.* New York: Crestwood House, Macmillan, 1990.

Parrot, Andrea, Ph.d. *Coping with Date Rape and Acquaintance Rape,* rev.ed. New York: Rosen Publishing Group, 1995.

Shuker-Haines, Frances. *Everything You Need to Know About Date Rape,* rev.ed. New York: Rosen Publishing Group, 1992.

Warshaw, Robin. *I Never Called It Rape.* New York: Harper and Row, 1988.

Index

About the Author

Maryann Miller has been published in numerous magazines and Dallas newspapers. She has served as editor, columnist, reviewer, and feature writer.

Married for over thirty years, Ms. Miller is the mother of five children. She and her husband live in Omaha, Nebraska.

Photo Credits

Cover photo and p. 36 by Michael Brandt; all other photos by Yung-Hee Chia.

Design by Blackbirch Graphics